JUDICIAL ACCOUNTABILITY

JUDICIAL ACCOUNTABILITY

Kalraj Mishra

Ocean Books Pvt. Ltd.
ISO 9001:2015 Publishers

Published by
Ocean Books (P) Ltd.
4/19 Asaf Ali Road,
New Delhi-110 002 (INDIA)
e-mail: info@oceanbooks.in

ISBN 978-81-8430-165-6
JUDICIAL ACCOUNTABILITY
by Shri Kalraj Mishra

Edition
2025

Price
₹ 250.00 (Rupees Two Hundred Fifty only)

Printed at
Print Media, New Delhi

To

MANANEEYA ATALJI

for his constant

Inspiration & Blessings

showered on me

"Nothing is to be done which creates even a suspicion that there has been an improper interference with the course of Justice."

—Lord Heward, Chief Justice Grain Brtown

"True Administration of Justice is the finest pillar of good government."

—George Washington

Contents

ARUN JAITLEY
Member of Parliament
Leader of Opposition
(Rajya Sabha)

सत्यमेव जयते

43, Parliament House
New Delhi - 11001
Tel: 23016707, 23034883
Fax: 23793433

Foreword

Shri Kalraj Mishra is a senior political leader. He has over five decades of public life behind him. Besides, being an important central and state functionary of the Bharatiya Janata Party, he has a strong legislative experience behind him. He has been a Member of the U.P. Legislative Council, Member of the Rajya Sabha on several occasions and is currently a Member of the Uttar Pradesh Legislative Assembly. This book conveys his insight as a political leader and a Legislator on the functioning of the judicial institution in India.

Judges discharge a divine function. They adjudicate disputes between ordinary human beings. There is thus a legitimate concern that the quality of the men who man the Indian judicial system must be of a high quality. The process of judicial appointments, the ability of judges to discharge their functions without fear or favour, ethics and scholarship are all important criterias which ensure a fair and powerful judiciary.

Besides, the selection of judges the manner in which judicial ethics are enforced is also a subject matter of public debate. The functioning of courts, the role of lawyers, litigants and witnesses require to be continuously debated so that the best possible system could be evolved. The evolution of laws particularly those relating to women are of prime concern to the society. This book is an evidence of high level of scholarship of Shri Kalraj Mishra and a compilation of his research and thoughts. I compliment him for this book.

New Delhi
9 February, 2013 **—Arun Jaitley**

Preface

The question of judicial independence and transparency in judicial appointment has remained a subject matter of public debate as well as a cause of concern over the past few years. Our Constitution has been amended several times to ensure a committed judiciary and even some times subjugating the judicial institution to function at the will of the executive. The other way the judicial independence was to strike at independent and impartial judges as we have seen the transfer of 16 judges of the High Court during emergency and supercession of seniormost judges in appointment as Chief Justice of India during 1971 and 1973.

Today we need an independent judiciary which is free from any pressure and can uphold the value of rule of law and restore public confidence in the institution of judiciary. But the true independence of judiciary and judicial activism has opened a new controversy. The power of struggle between the judiciary and executive has been tense. Our past experience shows that impeachment procedure for removal of corrupt judges as enshrined in the Constitution has really failed. The present study emphasizes on appointment of judges, inordinate delay in disposal of cases and judicial activism prevelant in the higher judiciairy. The study has also examined the other aspects, i.e appointment of judicial commission and appointment of retiring judges in government bodies just after their retirement.

I express my gratitutde to Vineet Ranjan a final year student of Amity Law School who has made untiring effort in making me available the necessary material. I also express my immense gratitude to the some of outstanding schlolars whose writings and views inspired me to undertake present study.

The book will be of interest to the people who wants to see an impartial and independent judiciary in the country. As a parliamentarian and as a Chairman of the Parliamentary Committee on Subordinate Legislation, I always realized the need for study on our judicial system which has been tarnished by incidents of increasing corruption in the government as well as in our judiciary. It has been extremely painful and distressing to note the fall of Indian judiciary in the estimation of all during last few years and thus requires introspection by each and every member of judiciary, executive, legislature and common people.

—Kalraj Mishra

(Former Chairman, Parliamentary
Committee on Subordinate Legislation)

Introduction

The Constitution of India has made elaborate provisions for ensuring independence of judiciary. The past experience of working of our Constitution shows that all is not working well with the judiciary. The blame for this state of affairs lies with all the organs of the state including the judiciary. The relationship between judiciary and executive has not been constant cordial. As a result, the institution of judiciary has suffered most and there has been constant deterioration in the quality of justice and judicial standards.

After Independence, the performance of the judiciary has come down under the close scrutiny. Apart from its criticism on account of lack of transparency, backlog of pending cases, controversial judgements and incidents of judicial activism has given the idea to explore the causes responsible for deterioration of judiciary and judicial accountability in India. The ambit of powers of the judiciary has created an expectation that the judiciary will exercise these powers judiciously, which has resulted into big debate whether the ample powers enshrined in our judicial system is being used judiciously.

While seeking the answer about the judicial accountability of judges, there are different views about lack of transparency in recruitment and appointment of judges and judicial decisions taken by our learned judges. There are many instances that the judicial appointment were made on the prerogative of executive. The glaring examples of such influence of executive over judiciary were seen in 1973 and 1977 when Justice Shelat and Justice H.R. Khanna were superceded by their juniors.

In view of the various corruption cases and various scams involving political personalities, every citizen of the country expects the judiciary to act firmly. It is possible only when judicial authority are allowed to function independently with judicious mind and ensures justice within a time frame work. There are three basic areas—fairness in term of appointment of judges, the question of delay in delivering the justice and judicial activism needs proper debate.

□

Mechanism for Selection and Appointment of Judges

A study of *Dharmshastras, Smritis* and *Arthshastra*[1] reveal that ancient India had a fairly well-developed system of administration of justice. The king was considered as the fountain of justice. In the discharge of his function, he was assisted by the Brahmins. Who were proficient in dharmshatras. For appointment of judges, Caste consideration was a dominant factor. Brahmins were preferred for judicial appointment.

As regards qualification, it was clearly laid down that the person should be proficient in the text; should be master of vedas and smritis and follow the path of *Dharma*. Women were not allowed to hold judicial office. Judge's tenure depended entirely on the pleasure of the king. In fact, the judges seemed to be more accountable to the king than to the people because their fate and future depended entirely on the pleasure of the king.

During 12th century, there was end of the Hindu period, Turkish race ruled Delhi for about 300 years and during this period judicial system was organized on the basis of administrative divisions of the kingdom and different courts were established at the central, provincial, district and *pargana* level (village level). All the courts functioned under the authority of the king with defined jurisdiction in civil, criminal and revenue matters. The entire judicial administration was headed by the sultan himself and all judicial appointments were made by him. But the process of removal was not as complicated as the impeachment procedure of today. Person of doubtful integrity were removed immediately from the office. Even a Chief Justice could be dismissed for want of honesty and on the ground of incompetency.

During 16th century, Mughal Rule was established and during this Period the Emperor was regarded as the fountain of justice. The Emperor established a seperate department of justice known as *Mahakme-Adalat*. Emperor's court was established in Delhi which was the highest judicial court exercising original and appellate jurisdiction. The Chief Justice and other puisne judges were appointed by the Emperor. Sometimes, the appointment were made from amongst the professional lawyers. Jadunath Sarkar has stated that "Men of high scholarship and reputed sanctity of character were appointed as judges. Judges of Subordinate court were preferably appointed from practicing lawyers. However, corrupt judges were not tolerated."[2]

Emperor Aurangzeb's order for appointing a person to occupy judicial office contained the following instruction: "Be honest, be impartial. Hold the trials in the presence of the parties and at the court house and the seat of the government. Do not accept present from the people of the place where you serve, nor attend the entertainment given by anybody and everybody...known poverty (*faqr*) to be your glory (fakhr)."[3]

Thus, during the Mughal Period, the quality of justice was very high. Only person possessing the required qualification could be considered for judicial appointment.

During British Period[4], there existed two sets of courts—the English people were governed by their own laws and courts whereas for the native population there were different courts. In other words, Presidency town of Madras, Bombay and Calcutta inhabited by the English and the *muffusil* areas dominated by rural population had different courts. During the period 1793-1861, some of the Governor-Generals showed a keen interest in improving the existing *Adalat* system by introducing many reforms.

The judges of the Supreme Court were appointed by the British Crown under his seal and held office during his pleasure. On the other hand, the judges of the Company's court were appointed by the Governor General and held office during his pleasure. Thus, the concept of "tenure and pleasure" made the judges subservient to the government, which means that the judges were accountable to the government while performing their judicial functions.

The Chartered Act of 1935 enacted by the British Parliament which centralized the whole legislative machinery and provided for appointment of law commission was a great step towards the unification of laws and courts. The enactment of Civil Procedure Code, Indian Penal Code and Criminal Procedure Code in the years 1859, 1860 1861 respectively paved the way for the amalgamation of the dual system of courts and finally the object was achieved by Indian High Court Act, 1861.

In August 1861 by enactment of Indian High Court Act, Her Majesty was empowered to abolish the Supreme Court and *sadar adalats* and in their place constitute a High Court of judicature for each of the three Presidencies. The court was to consist of a Chief Justice and such other number of judges to be appointed by Her Majesty from time to time.[5] The act prescribed professional qualification of judges and the judges were appointed by Her Majesty and held office during Her Majesty, pleasure.

The enactment of the Government of India Act, 1935 gave a new dimension to the judicial system of the country. The act for the first time guaranteed a security of tenure to the judges who could be removed by His Majesty only on the ground of proved misbehavior or infirmity of mind or body. It was a drastic change as judges from 1862 to 1935 used to hold office during Her Majesty pleasure. Whereas from 1935 they held office during good behavior and also special provisions were made for salary and pension of judges.

The other significant provision of the Government of India Act 1935 related to the creation of Federal Court in India. On 1st October 1937, the Federal Court consisting of Chief Justice and two puisne Judges was established at Delhi. The judges of the Federal Court were to be appointed by the British crown and they were to hold office until they attained the age of 65 years. However, a judge could resign or be removed earlier on the ground of misbehavior or of a mental or physical infirmity if the privy council on the reference by the Crown so recommended.[6]

The Federal Court continued to function even after India attained Independence in 1947 till its jurisdiction was taken over by present Supreme Court under the Constitution of 1950.

When the Constituent Assembly started its work, the most difficult and daunting task was to make provision for an independent and impartial judiciary in the country. This was sought to be ensured through the procedure for appointment of judges and a fixed term for them. It is unanimously agreed that every effort should be made to keep politics out of judicial corridors. Neither the executive nor the Chief Justice of India have a final say in making judicial appointments. By an large the framers of the Constitution were contended by conferring wide appellate, original as well as writ jurisdiction on the High Court and the Supreme Court so that they could effectively deliver justice to the people of this great country.

□

Judicial Appointments Under Constitution

In the Constitution, Article 124 deals with the appointment of judges in the Supreme Court and Article 217 regarding appointment of the judges to the High Court emerged after considerable discussion and debate in the Constituent Assembly[7]. Articles 124 to 147 in Chapter IV Part V of the constitution under the caption "union judiciary" deals with the establishment and constitution of Supreme Court, the appointment of judges and their powers, rights, jurisdiction and their service conditions including transfer from one High Court to other.

Though the constitutional provisions in Articles 124 and 217 are seemingly simple and unambiguous, yet it has given rise to different interpretations on three different occasions since last two decades by the Supreme Court to decide the question of correct selection process.

The verdicts in *S.P. Gupta* vs. *Union of India,*[8] *S.C. Advocate on Record* vs. *Union of India*[9] and the Presidential reference no. 1 of 1998(1991) 7 SCC 739 has given rise to a constant debate about the efficacy of the methods of appointment of the judges of the higher judiciary by the existing procedure and the need to set up a national judicial commission. There have been decisions of the Apex Court wherein the present system of appointment of judges is found efficacious and perserves the independence of judiciary.

On 26 October 1991 in a PIL titled *Subhash Sharma* vs. *Union of India,*[10] the three judges bench referred the matter to a larger bench for the following question—

1. Whether the opinion of the Chief Justice of India in regard to the appointment of judges to the Supreme Court and High Court as well as in regard to the transfer of judges is entitled to primacy.
2. Whether the matter including the fixation of strength of judges in the High Court are justiciable.

The procedure followed till then in the field of selection and appointment of judges exclusively vested with the executive which could even ignore the recommendation of Chief Justice of India. The decision in *S.P. Verma* vs. *Union of India* put judicial stamp of approval. This caused great harm to the judicial institution and resulted into excessive politicization of judiciary. As we have seen in 1973 and 1977 the supercession of two senior judges-Justice Shelat and Justice H.R. Khanna in appointment as Chief Justice of India.

The nine judge bench of the Supreme Court of India made the following conclusions—

(i) The process of appointment of judges to the Supreme Court and High Court is an integrated participatory process for selecting the best and most suitable persons and all constitutional functionaries must perform this duty collectively with a view primarily to reach an agreed decision, subserving the constitutional purpose, so that the occasion of primacy does not arise.

(ii) Initiation of the proposal, for appointment in case of Supreme Court, must be by the Chief Justice of India and in case of High Court the proposal has to be initiated by the Chief Justice of High Court.

(iii) In the event of conflicting opinion by the constitutional functionaries, the opinion of Chief Justice of India has primacy.

(iv) No appointment of any judge to the Supreme Court or any High Court can be made, unless it is in conformity with the opinion of the Chief Justice of India.

(v) Appointment of the Chief Justice of India should be of the senior most judge of the Supreme Court.

(vi) The opinion of the Chief Justice of India has not mere primacy but is determined in the matter of transfer of High Court judges.

(vii) In making all appointments and transfers, the norms indicated must be followed, however, the same do not confer any rights in anyone.

(viii) Fixation of judge strength in the High Court is justiciable but only to the extent and in manner indicated.

In view of the contrary decision in two cases, the President of India, in exercise of his power under Article 143(1) of the Constitution, referred in July 1998. The question in the President reference related broadly the three aspects—

(a) Consultation between the Chief Justice and his brother judges, in the matter of appointment of judges of the Supreme Court and High Court and transfer of High Court judges.
(b) Judicial review of transfer of judges.
(c) The relevance of seniority in making the appointment to the Supreme Court.

The nine judges special reference constitution bench accordingly answered the question asked in President reference.

1. The term 'consultation with Chief Justice of India in Articles 217(1) and 222(1)' requires consultation with majority of judges in formation of opinion of the Chief Justice of India. The individual opinion of Chief Justice of India does not constitute consultation within the meaning of said article.
2. The transfer of judges can be reviewed only when the recommendation made by the Chief Justice of India has not been made in consultation with the four senior most judges of Supreme Court or that the opinion of Chief Justice of concerned High Court have not been obtained.

3. 'Strong cogent reason' do not have to be recorded as a justification for departure for the order of seniority rather the positive reasons for the recommendation violating the seniority should be recorded.
4. The recommendation made by the Chief Justice of India without complying with the norms and requirement of the consultation process are not binding upon the Government of India.[11]

In view of the contradictory interpretation on these three occasions, recommendation for collegium was expressed by many jurist. Justice P.N Bhagwati who delivered the main judgement in first judge case made for a collegiums for making a recommendation to The President.

Earlier former Chief Justice Y.B. Chandrachud in 1983 in a seminar at Patna recommended for burial of the system of recommendation adopted at that time.

Recently, committee on judicial accountability prepared a draft bill for amendment to the constitution providing for the National Judicial Commission. In their manifesto N.D.A. mentioned for the creation of National Judicial Commission which will recommend judicial appointment in higher judiciary.

There are many conflicting views expressed on the matter. Shri K.P.S. Gill, former D.G.P., criticises the second judge transfer case and argues that India is the only country in the world where judges select themselves, determine their own transfers and discipline themselves. He recommended for setting up of a judicial commission which would be responsible not only for appointment and transfer of Judges but also to see that judges perform their duties properly without any favour of face.[12]

In a discussion in Rajya Sabha on Librahan Commission report former Law Minister and Leader of Opposition, Shri Arun Jaitley expressed his views that there are two types of judges "one who knows law and second who knows the law minister". The opinion expressed by the Shri Arun Jaitley strengthens the allegation that the influence of executive in appointment of judges cannot be ruled out unless a judicial commission is formed.

Recently, the Chief Justice of India has written to the law ministry that in case of corruption against a judge of Supreme Court/High Court, it is important for judiciary to conduct its own probe before the matter is handed over to any agency (CBI/police). In this way, the remarks of Chief Justice of India is against the principal of separation power.[13]

On 30/9/2012 BJP President Shri Nitin Gadkari called for a two-year cooling off period before a judge is considered for post-retirement post. The present system adversely affects the independence of judiciary vis-à-vis the government. He put that there is growing tendency among several judges, on the verge of retirement, try to speak and act friendly to the government with an eye on crushy governmental assignment just after retirement.[14]

On the same occasion, former Law Minister and Leader of Opposition Shri. Arun Jaitley articulated that this clamor for post-retirement jobs is adversely affecting the impartiality.

Commenting on judicial accountability, Shri. Prashant Bhushan, Sr. Advocate in Supreme Court has favoured for National Judicial Council to enquire the complaints against judges is being perceived as a long awaited initiative to introduce some accountability for judges of the higher judiciary.[15]

While referring Ramaswami's case of late 1980's, he says that Ramaswami was tried by a committee of three judges and was found guilty of many charges but he could not be removed by impeachment because ruling party decided to abstain from voting on his impeachment motion.

According to Shri. Shanti Bhushan, the problem of judicial accountability has been compounded by the Supreme Court's judgement in the *Veeraswami's case,* in which the Supreme Court held that no judges of the High Court or Supreme Court could be subjected to even investigation if any offence of corruption otherwise unless one obtain prior written permission of Chief Justice of India. This has resulted in a situation whereby no sitting judge has been subjected to even investigation in the last 15 years since that judgement, despite public knowledge and complaint of widespread corruption in judiciary. The police does not dare to approach the Chief Justice for permission to investigate the charges labelled against a judge unless they already have clinching evidence, which they cannot get unless they investigate.

Further the judiciary is even insulated from public criticism by the threat of contempt of court which can be used in a very draconian manner by the very judges towards whom the criticism is directed as we saw in the Arundhati Roy case.

Surprisingly, the Supreme Court by a amazing creating interpretation of the constitution has taken over the power of appointing judges.

The words appointed by the President in consultation with Chief Justice of India in the constitution was interpreted as appointed by the government (President) on advice of the Chief Justice of India.

In a news published in *Times of India,* Chief Justice of India compounded The Union Government's difficulties on Judicial standard and Accountability Bill by warning that hasty steps may affect the judicial independence. Justice Kapadia lamented that in the name of the judicial accountability, the independence of judiciary cannot be compromised.

Thus, the lack of will of the government of India and fear of higher judiciary is basically responsible for the situation which has now taken place in absence of transparency in our judicial system.

□

Delay in Delivering Justice

It is old saying that 'justice delayed is justice denied'. In India, speedy justice is always been *sine quo non* of criminal jurisprudence. Mr. D.P. Sharma in his article "Speedy Justice and Indian Criminal Justice System"[16] has stated that speedy justice is one of the key elements of reform in the Indian system particularly in Indian criminal system. According to him, it is an important safeguard to prevent undue and oppressive incarnation. The right of speedy justice has been actuated in recent past. The courts in many decision have opened new vistas of fundamental right. The right to speedy trial is an integral part of fundamental right to life and liberty enshrined under Article. 21 of the Constitution. In *A.R. Antulay* vs. *R.S. Nayak,* the constitutional bench of Supreme Court held that right to speedy trial is implicit in Article 21 of the Constitution.

In *Hussainara Khatoon* vs. *Home Secretary, State of Bihar,*[17] the Supreme Court held that now obviously procedure prescribed by law for depriving a person of his liberty cannot be reasonable, fair or just unless that procedure ensures a speedy trial for determination of the guilt of such person. No procedure which does not ensure a reasonably quick trial can be regarded as reasonable, fair and just and would fall of Article 21. There can, therefore, be no doubt that by speedy trial we mean reasonably expeditious trial, is an integral and essential part of the fundamental right to life and liberty enshrined in Article 21.

Right to speedy trial begins with he actual restraint imposed by arrest and consequent incarnation and continues at all stages, namely the investigation, inquiry, trial and appeal. In this context, it may be noted that the constitutional guarantee of speedy trial is properly reflected in section 309 of Code of Criminal Procedure.

There have been various committees to look after the delay in disposal of cases but still there is huge arrears of pending cases in the High Court as well as Supreme Court. Some of the committees are—

(a) Rankin Committee was formed in 1924 to look after the reason of delay in disposal of civil cases in High Court and lower courts.
(b) High Court Arrears Committee (1949) was formed with the aim of advisability of curtailing of right of appeal and revision to reduce the accumulation of arrears.
(c) Review committee of 1967 and 1969 were to conduct and suggest ways for reducing arrears of pending cases in the High Courts.
(d) Arrears Committee (1990) was formed to identify various causes for accumulation of arrears of pending cases in the High Court. Arrears Committee (1993) formed to suggest remedial measures for reducing the arrears of criminal cases.

All these committees made valuable suggestions and recommendations to provide speedy and fair justice to accused person.

National Police Commission had made suggestions for improvement in criminal justice system. It suggested the ways by reducing the institution of fresh cases, withdrawing old cases from courts according to some accepted norms and expediting the disposal of pending cases by simplifying the procedure. But unfortunately the court still work on the basis of 100 yrs old procedure and judge seldom make efforts to reduce the arrears of pending cases.

The Law Commission made several suggestions and recommendations in the past, i.e. 32nd report on section 9 of Cr.P.C. (1967), 33rd report on Section 44 of Cr.P.C. (1967), 37th report on Sections 1 to 176 of Cr.P.C. (1967), 41st report on the Code of Criminal Procedure(1969) to remove anomalies, ambiguity of the criminal justice process and to suggest ways and means of speedy trials and avoiding delays.

In views of the recommendations made by the law commissions, the new Code of Criminal Procedure, 1973 has been enacted taking into consideration the need for speeding the disposal of criminal cases. Sections 167, 309 and 468 of the new Code of Criminal Procedure, 1973 synthesize the certain changes particularly in respect of speedy trial and elimination of delays in investigation and trial proceeding.

While dealing with the question of delay and arrears in criminal cases, the Law Commission of India, in its 77th report on delay and arrears in trial courts made some recommendations which are detailed below—

1. In criminal matters the delay be eliminated since the decision is based on oral rather than documentary evidence and with the passage of time, the memory of witness fades.
2. The tendency of some courts of sending back witnesses without examining them must be deprecated.
3. The law should be amended to enable a session judge to act on evidence partly or wholly recorded by his predecessors.
4. The police act more promptly to ensure the serving of summons of witnesses and ensuring their presence on date of hearing.
5. The trial magistrate should not leave it to the prosecutor to the charges.
6. In recording statement of the accused under Section., 313 Cr.P.C. the magistrate should ensure that all incrimating pieces of evidence are put to the accused.
7. Cases in which there is a possibility of death sentence should receive priority over all other cases.

There are many recommendations submitted by the Law Commissions from time to time. But the need of the hour is to incorporate them in action plans to see that these become a part of actual practices by the functioning courts dealing with criminal cases.

According to Shri S.M.N. Raina, former Judge of M.P. High Court, only judges are often criticized for delay in disposal of cases. This is mainly due to the system under they are required to work and other factors over which they have no control. Judges contribution to the delay is usually due to the following reasons—

1. Fixing to many cases for evidence on a particular day with the result that some of them are adjourned.
2. Loose handling of a case by not promptly disposing of all interlocutor applications and granting adjournment without any justification whatsoever.
3. Prolonged arguments which the judge could curtail by intelligent and effective intervention.
4. Fixing the case for rehearing without any justification after the case has been fully heard.
5. Delay in delivering judgement.

But as per my opinion such delay can be avoided by a judge by exercising effective control on the proceeding throughout. In order to make justice speedy, the entire system of administration of justice particularly the procedural law needs to be overhauled.

Looking to the large number of pending cases in different courts, the emphasis on disposal is quite natural and it is the duty of the judge to ensure that they are disposed of as expediously as possible. But it must be kept in mind that the court sits to decide a case in order to administer justice and merely to dispose it of in undue haste should therefore be avoided. In other words, the judge can be expected to do is to work in court sincerely and with devotion throughout the court hours.

Quick disposal of case is good but it should not be at the cost of justice. The delay in cases would render the entire proceeding infructuous[19].

Justice Shelat also made a similar observation in his address on the subject 'Judiciary vis-à-vis Society—

"At the same time it is equally reasonable to think that decision hurridly given by any court defeats real justice and gives no satisfaction to the parties affected. While speedy and quick administration of justice is highly desirable, it should not be done so hurridly to defeat the purpose."

T.P. Kelu, Sr. Advocate of Kerela High Court in his article states about a true judge and people's expectation from him.[20] It is wrong to assume that a person becomes eligible to enjoy the so-called majesty of office, its powers and privileges. A judge is not a mere terminator of litigation rather he is a generator of justice. The article restraints the judges to act to catch the eyes of the newsman. In the present day, ordinarily judges decide easy cases but hard cases they bring into moses.

The Supreme Court in its decision in *Hussainara Khatoon*[21] brought to light a shocking state of affairs of our legal and judicial system. The Court discovered that thousands of men, women and children were languishing in jail for years awaiting trial. The result in the case resulted in the release of more than ,22,000 under trial prisoners. There are many reason for delay—

1. Failure of the state to give due priority to judicial matters including the appointment of judges.
2. Writ jurisdiction of High Court and style of its exercise is resulting into inordinate delay.
3. The Senior lawyers in whose hands most of the work fall contribute to delay and arrears by their non-availability and unpreparedness.

Chief Justice P.N. Bhagwati also expressed his disappointment in the last vacant day speech in November 1986 and accused the government for its inaction in appointment and disregarding the recommendation of judges.

The problem has to be solved without any further delay as the judiciary is almost on the brink of collapse. The process of rejudicialisation is on, the administrative tribunal act and legal service act are the latest instance of the curtailment of courts jurisdiction. Therefore, the solution is not to deny justice to the people but to introduce some innovative changes in the judicial system so as to keep pace with the growth of the litigation in the country. The earlier we do it, it would be better in the interest of justice.

As per the report of *Hindustan Times* dated 20/8/2012, the final hearing of the case started after 37 years of after assassination of Former Railway Minister Shri. L.N. Mishra in 1974 in a bomb blast at Samastipur Junction. A Delhi Court is set to hear final argument in the case. If a minister cannot get justice in a span of 37 years, how can the common people get justice in this judicial system. According to the information provided by the law ministry as on 31/12/2011 around 43 lakhs cases are pending in different High Courts.

□

Judicial Activism in India

The third basic area in addition to the fairness and transperancy in appointment of judges/delay in providing justice is the problem of judicial activism which needs to be probed to give clear view on the judicial accountability in India. The concept of committed judiciary was imported to our system in 1973 when Chief Justice Sikri retired and the hunt for the next successor had just started. Mrs. Indira Gandhi the then Prime Minister propounded the theory of committed judiciary. She expressed the view that the independent India should have judges who are committed not only to the social philosophy of the Constitution but also to the government. The theory started the tendency of judicial activism in the country when the judges normally exceed the judicial limits.

On speaking on the occasion of 150th anniversary of Madras High Court, President Shri Pranab Mukherjee urged judiciary to temper its activism lest it disturb the principle of separation of power enshrined in the Constitution. He further stated that the judicial activism should not lead to erosion of constitutional principal of separation of power. The only check on judiciary is self-restraint. Commenting on independence of judiciary must be preserved at all costs. Justice must be quick and accessible to all. Welcoming the new initiative like the National Mission of Justice delivering and the proposed All India Judicial Service. He also emphasized that selection and appointment of judges should conform to the highest standard.[22]

R.K. Jain, Senior advocate in Supreme Court, says that judicial activism signifies performance by the judiciary of some functions which do not strictly fall in the domain of jurisdiction of judiciary and which ought to have been performed by other wings of the state. In fact, it is an innovative measure initiated by Supreme Court towards attaining constitutionally-oriented objective in the form of public interest litigation. Though some people think it is a mean of doing justice to the helpless silent majority who cannot approach to the court for justice.

Our Constitution embodied the doctrine of separation of powers of the three organs of the state. Broadly speaking, the function of Parliament is to enact laws and of the executive is to execute and comply with the laws so enacted. The function of the judiciary is to oversee and ensure that the Constitution and laws are obeyed. Thus, the power of judicial review given by the Constitution to the judiciary make the task of judiciary of paramount importance.

Later on with the passage of time, the judiciary realized that many people can't get justice because of poverty, illiteracy, social backwardness. The court therefore modified the principle of *locus standi* so that the under-privileged can get justice. Perhaps this was first time a crucial step was taken by judiciary in ensuring and taking justice to the door step of the poor. While addressing the deep-rooted problem of corruption in high offices, i.e 2G Spectrum scandal, CWG scam and other corruption cases, the hon'ble Supreme Court had showed that " Be you howsoever high, the law is always above you".

Even the matter of abolition of child labour, prison reform and taking action against erring industries, in the matter of pollution, the judiciary had to intervene. In other words judicial activism is the need of the day.

Though there is another view that activist approach of judiciary is not healthy for democratic system. The judiciary is overstepping its limits by adopting the activist approach. Though the people of India has immense faith and trust in the judicial system. As the President in his address has rightly warned of the consequences of judicial activism because in a democracy the doctrine of separation of power should be adopted in a honest manner.

Justice H.R. Khanna once said "when the light of law fails, judges are suppose to have special vision like the third eye of Shiva...they may solve enigmas that no other agency of the government has been able to solve". But on the question of judicial activism, he said "judges ought not to be seduced by the quitic temptation to encroach upon other field.... The court have to be much more circumspect in seeing that they do not overstep the limits of their power. The special responsibility of the court to ensure that one wing of state does not intrude upon the fields of others, make it essential for the judges to avoid an over activist role."[23]

The critics assert that the judicial activism has resulted in the courts issuing direction to the government agencies, local bodies, police departments, environment authorities, industries, even officials in many matters, which amounted to uprising the function of administrative agencies. It is normally argued that such decisions often land the administration in practical difficulties and make them bear the brunt of these decisions. Some of which are considered to be based on inadequate appreciation of administrative requirements and compulsions about which the courts sometimes do not possess requisite administrative expertise and proficiency.

The former Chief Justice of India Justice A.M. Ahmedi had once described Supreme Court as the world's most powerful court because of its wide ranging vast jurisdiction apart from its original, appellate and advisory jurisdiction. It has the power to entertain petitions even from ordinary people who otherwise cannot approach it due to financial and other problems.

Former Chief Justice P.N. Bhagwati propounded in *S.P. Gupta's case*: "The Court has to innovate new methods and devise new strategies for the purpose of providing access to justice to large masses of people who are denied their basic human rights. The only way in which this can be done is by entertaining Writ Petitions and even letter from public spirited citizens seeking judicial redress on behalf of those who have suffered a legal wrong or an injury."

It may be wrong to assume that judicial activism results in judicial oligarchy dethrowing democratic supremacy. But the doctrine of separation of power should be followed by all the organs of democratic system. Even after 63 years of independence we have miles to go and promises to keep we cannot sleep till we wipe out the tears from the eyes of the poorest to poor. This is what is being attempted through judicial activism instead of judicial activism it may be termed as judicial humanism.

□

The Judges (Inquiry) Bill 2006 vis-a-vis Judicial Standards and Accountability Bill

By the virtue of public pressure and principal stand taken by certain judges and one ruling by the Delhi High Court has compelled public disclosure of assets by judges. But this is not certainly the end of the serious problem of lack of judicial accountability. The main issue is the absence of an independent credible institution which could entertain complaints against judges, investigate them and take action against errant members of the bench." In this complex situation, recently the Govt. of India has come up with the Judges (Inquiry) Bill 2006 to address this problem of unaccountability by the members of judiciary for any kind of misconduct committed on their part.[24]

To make judiciary more accountable by arming any person with the right to file a complaint against judges of higher judiciary for their misconduct or inefficiency, the Judges (Inquiry) Bill, 2006 was introduced in Lok Sabha. It has proposed to make some necessary amendments in the existing Judges (Inquiry) Act, 1968. As we have seen that the provisions of act of 1968 were insufficient as experienced in *Justice V. Ramaswami's case* who was a sitting judge in the Apex Court.

The Bill of 2006 provides for establishment of a National Judicial Council consisting of sitting judges to undertake—

1. Preliminary investigation and inquiry into allegation of misbehavior/miscount against a judge of higher judiciary.
2. Regulate the procedure for such investigation, inquiry and proof.
3. For imposing minor measures.
4. Presentation of an address by Parliament to the President for removal of judge.[25]

The National Council consists of the following in the matter pertaining to judge of High Court—

1. Chair Person—Chief Justice of India.
2. Two senior most judges of Supreme Court as members.
3. Two Chief Justices of High Courts as members (all members are nominated by Chief Justice of India).

In case of a complaint against a judge of Supreme Court, the National Council consists of—

1. Chairman—Chief Justice of India
2. Members—Four senior most Supreme Court judges nominated by Chief Justice of India.

The Bill provides that any person can make a complaint of allegation of misbehavior or incapacity irrespect of a judge to the Council provided that no such complaint shall be entertained and inquired into with respect to any act or conduct constituting misbehavior which has taken place before the commencement of this act and also any act which has taken place two years prior to the date of filing the complaint. It also provides that no complaint shall be entertained against a person who has demitted the office of the judge. If after the inquiry the council comes to the conclusion that the charges have been proved, it may impose all or any one of the minor penalties, if the charges do not warrant removal of the judge:

1. Issuing advisories
2. Warnings
3. Withdrawal of judicial work for limited time
4. Request the judge to take voluntary retirement
5. Censure or abomination

In case the Council comes to the conclusion that the serious nature charge warrants the removal of judge concerned, the Council shall advise the judge accordingly. In case of reference, the Bill enshrines the same procedure envisaged under the Act of 1968.

The Act of 1968 provides that in case a notice is given of a motion for presenting an address to the President for praying for removal of judge on ground of misbehavior or incapacity (in case of notice is given in Lok Sabha by not less than 100 members of Lok Sabha and in case notice given Rajya Sabha not less than 50 members of that House) then the Speaker/Chairman may after considering the matter admit or reject the motion. If the motion is admitted then the Speaker or the Chairman as the case may be shall keep the motion pending and refer all allegations to the Council. The council shall hold the inquiry and forward its report to the speaker/chairman. If the charges are proved and warrants removal, then the motion along with the Council's report shall be taken up for consideration by the House of the Parliament in which it is pending.

In case the motion is adopted in accordance with the provision Clause (4) of Article 124 of the Constitution, then the misbehavior or incapacity of the judges shall be deemed have been proved and express address praying for removal of judge shall be presented to the President by each House of Parliament.

The Bill also provides for provision of an appeal by the aggrieved judge to the Supreme Court in case of order of removal is passed by the President or against a final order passed by the Council imposing any of the minor measures.

The Bill also makes certain provision for code of conduct and behavior of judges, empowering the council to issue guidelines from time to time. Bill also contains provisions for disclosure of assets and liabilities by judges at the time of appointment and thereafter annually and any violation of code of conduct would come within the ambit of misbehavior and lastly the Judges Inquiry Bill, 2006 will repeal the Judges (Inquiry) Act, 1968.

An Appraisal of Judges (Inquiry) Bill 2006

The Bill aims to bring accountability in the judiciary which till day was considered beyond the pale of any effective legal regime. In the history of the country first time the sweeping reforms are being introduced to make judiciary more accountable and to check alleged corruption in our judicial system. In fact, the judicial reforms are due for long time and the accountability being major concern under the category of reforms has found full attention in the Bill which is truly in a right direction.[26]

The Bill comprises 38 Sections and divided into IX Chapters aims to look into allegation of misconduct brought forth against the judges of the higher judiciary. As compared to the previous legislation on the subject, the Bill of 2006 is quite comprehensive and has tried to remove ambiguity which was present in the earlier legislation. The Bill has tried to define the misbehavior in right perspective. In Section 2(J), the term 'misbehavior' has been defined as "willful or persistent conduct which brings dishonor or disrespect to the judiciary or willful or persistent failure to perform the duties of a judge or willful misuse of judicial office". Corruption, lack of integrity, committing an offence involving moral turpitude and includes violation of code of conduct. The definition is wide enough and inclusive. By including the violation of code of conduct within the parameters of misbehavior, it has injected life into the values of our judicial system. The Bill of 2006 has introduced the complaint procedure as well as the reference procedure. The provision has excluded the Chief Justice of India from the complaint procedure as well as from the reference procedure which has already evoked strong and different reaction from all the corners. The said Bill contains enough provisions to discourage frivolous complaints on the merit of the judgement as a procedural order. The Bill has empowered the National judicial commission for dismissal of such complaints.

2006 Bill is being perceived as good initiative to introduce some accountability for judges of higher judiciary.

Judicial behavior received attention in 1998 when a former judge of the Supreme Court observed that everything was rotten about the Indian judiciary.[27] A spate of scam involving judges in bribery, corruption and misuse of judicial office and deviation from constitutional values are indicating a very harsh reality. At present except the removal procedure prescribed under Article 124(4) of the Constitution, there is no institutionalized mechanism to investigate complaints against the judges.

In the Judges Inquiry Bill (2006), the complained can be filed against judges of the Supreme Court and High Court before the Council. But no complaint can be made against the Chief Justice of India. The charges against the Chief Justice of India can be probed by a reference which requires at least 100 members in Lok Sabha and 50 members in Rajya Sabha. Former Chief Justice of India Justice J.S. Verma said that the Chief Justice of India should be under judicial council and has expressed that when the CJI and all other judges are alike then the Chief Justice of India should not be exempted from the complaint procedure.[28]

In the Judicial Standard and Accountability Bill, 2010 which has been passed in Lok Sabha and to be submitted in Rajya Sabha, there is a provision which seeks to debar judges from making oral comments in courts and the government of India has refused to delete this provision. But the government has wrongly interpreted the recent Supreme Court judgement and SC's response to the Presidential reference in 2G Spectrum that the policy decision making is and should remain in the executive domain, to effect that the theory of separation of power does not take away the duty of Supreme Court to protect the Constitution and ensure the Rule of law. The constitution provides equal opportunity to all citizens and the executive cannot allow pick and choose on the name of policy decision which they have done in allocation of 2G Spectrum.

□

Role of Different Organs of Judicial System

(A) Role of Judges

In delivering justice, judges can be broadly classified into two categories, namely Conservative Judges and Liberal Judges. A conservative judge takes the law as it is and prefers to follow the beaten track. He performs his judicial functions regardless of the consideration whether his decision causes undue hardships to the litigant. For a conservative judge, justice is merely synonym for what is lawful and this type of justice is known as technical justice.

A liberal judge, on the other hand, is primarily concerned with doing justice. He too has to justice as per the law but he tries to find ways to mitigate the rigourisity of law to avoid a hardship to the party in litigation. Thus, while in conservative justice, a judge is merely concerned with deciding the case according to the law whereas a liberal judge finds ways and means to do substantial justice taking care that his decision does not violate against the law. For example, under Article 226 of the Constitution, some judges dismiss the petition on the ground that on alternate remedy is available to the litigant whereas other judges grant relief in spite of availability of alternate remedy. Some judges would insist on strict adherence to the rule, regardless of its consequences. Similarly, the approach of two kinds of judges is entirely different in the matter of using discretionary power. One makes efforts to promote justice while the other is simply to dispose of the case on technical grounds.

Justice M.C. Chagla who has known to be a liberal judge has indicated in his book *Roses in December* that "I started with trying to find out where justice lay or what a common sense view would dictate. I fully realized that in a court we administer justice according to the law and not abstract justice. But to the extent that I could fit in the law with justice without undue distortion, I would do so" (p. 158).

A liberal judge is aware that he has to do justice according to the law but should keep in mind that his decision should not go against the existing law.

In this connection I would like to mention that almost in every case the judge reaches at a conclusion then he records his decision on the basis of supportive reasons and evidence and cites authorities in support of his conclusion and I think most of the judges function in this way. In other words, a judge cannot write a judgement without making up his mind one way or the other way. If there is a precedent supporting his stand he would record it. If it does not support the view, he would find a way to distinguish it or to say that the said precedent is not binding on him relying on the doctrine of *per incurian, sub silenta* etc.

It would be pertinent to mention that the scope of the subordinate judiciary to do justice is confined to the facts of the case. By pick and chose method, they made the law the way it suits them whereas they are supposed to exist themselves to get the truth by taking an intelligent and sustained interest in the trial of the case from beginning to end. The judicial power is usually concerned with the adjudication of disputes and providing justice. The judges are not supposed to function merely following the theory of technical justice. In his lecture on judicial process Chief Justice M. Hidayatullah observed that "the prerogative writs do more than establish a rule of law; they provide means to prescribe administrative behaviour, which is true sociological approach to law. By their decisions, the judge become the architect of the society".

The courts in course of their functions have to reconcile the demands of a welfare state with the rule of law, though it is a very delicate task. A statute made by the legislative does not speak for itself. It is the judge which listens the voice of the statute and expounds its meaning. The judge breathes life in a statute and shape it in accordance with the intention of the legislature to make it effective instrument of justice. Thus, the primary responsibility of our learned judges is to provide justice and not merely deciding disputes in a mechanical way. By doing this they can reduce the backlog of pending case which has piled up a lot.

The Judges should have the Following Qualities

Speedy and satisfactory disposal of cases depends on competence of judges. The judge's should be men of character and integrity. They should be well versed in law. Shukraniti (Ch. IV-5-15-1 8) says—

व्यवहारविद : प्राज्ञा वृतशील गुणाविंता: ।
रिपो नित्रे समा ये च धर्मज्ञास्सत्य वदित: ॥
निरालसता जित क्रोध, काम, लोभ: प्रियंवक्ष ।
राज्ञा नियोजित व्यास्ते सम्यास्सर्वासु जातिषु ॥

"One who is well versed in civil and criminal law and procedure, sprightful, of starling character, impartial towards friends and foes, of *Dharma* abiding nature, truthful, ever active and who has established control over anger, desire and greed and pleasant in speech and demeanor should be appointed a judge."

***Manusmriti* says—**

पिताचार्य सुद्धमान्ता भार्या पुत्र पुरोहिता: ।
नादण्डेया नाम राक्षैस्ति य स्वधेर्म न तिष्ठिति ॥

"He should not leave an offender unpunished whatever may be his relationship with him. Neither father nor a teacher, nor a friend, nor mother, nor wife, nor a son nor a domestic priest should go unpunished for the offence committed."

About the qualification and duties of judge's *Atrismriti* (28) says—

दुवटस्य दण्ड : सुजनस्य पूजा ।
न्यायेन कोषस्य च संपवृद्धि ॥
अपथपातो र्थिषु राष्ट्र रक्षा ।
पच्चैव यज्ञा: कथिता नृपाणाम ॥

"To punish the wicked, to protect the good, to enrich the treasury by just methods, to render justice impartially to the litigants and to protect the kingdom. These are five *yagnas* to be performed."

In *Shukraniti* (Ch. V-14-15), it is stated—

पक्षपाताधिरोपस्य कारणानि च पच्चवै।
रागलोभभयद्वेषा वादिनोश्च रहरश्रुति॥

"There are five causes which give rise to the charge of partiality. They are 1. Raga (affection); 2. Lobh (greed); 3. Bhaya (fear); 4. Dwesha (ill will); and 5. Vadinoscha Raharshruti (meeting and hearing secretly)."

***Narada Smriti* says—**

यात्यचोरोचिचोरत्वं चोरश्चात्य चोरताम।
अचोश्चोरता प्राप्तो भाण्डव्यो व्यवहारतः॥

"One who has not committed theft or robbery may be found guilty of the offence. An actual thief or robber on the other hand may be acquitted of the charge. Mandavya (an ascetic who has innocent) was tried and declared to be guilty. Hence, judges must be extremely careful in delivering justice."

□

(B) Role of Lawyers in Providing Justice

The lawyer is extremely important and valuable in the administration of justice. His assistance is very valuable to a judge while delivering justice. The justice may be defeated if the lawyer fails to perform his function well. Their learning in the bar is reflected in the judgments of the courts and the contribution of lawyers to jurisprudence is in no way less important than to that of a judge. Although the lawyers are generally indifferent to justice, I have seen many lawyers readily responding to the consideration of justice and helping the court in delivering real and substantial justice. While during arguments, each lawyer makes effort to have a decision in favor of his client but if the judge indicates a talk on consideration of justice, I have seen many lawyers assisting the judge in arriving at a just conclusion, even though it may not suit its client. A lawyer should always keep in mind of his solemn duty to advance the cause of justice and not merely the interest of his client.

Unfortunately, in modern times the lawyers have forgotten their solemn duty and are primarily concerned with the interest of their clients. They care little for jurisprudence.

In famous BMW case famous lawyer and a former member of Rajya Sabha Shri R.K. Anand was found guilty of adopting malafide practice in order to facilitate his client by manipulating the main eyewitness along with famous criminal lawyer U.A. Khan which was against the solemn duty of advocate and he was banned from legal practice and was imposed fine also.

This unexpected conduct of an advocate of stature of Shri. R.K. Anand is an unfortunate and unforgettable incidence of Indian Judicial System. In another incident in an interview on 28/11/2012 on a famous T.V Channel Shri. Ram Jethmalani former Law Minister of the country who had been four times President of Bar Council of India admitted that in our legal profession it is our prime objective to ensure the interest of client rather assisting the court in reaching a just decision Majority of lawyers are doing the same. Either they prolong the case by taking the adjournment on false plea or purely on technical considerations, which is resulting into backlog of pending cases in higher judiciary as well as in subordinate judiciary. As a Member Parliament several times I have taken up the matter with Govt. of India but all the efforts have gone in vain. I got several assurances from Law Ministry but nothing was done. In fact, it is the bar which can bring the large number of pending cases in Supreme Court and in different High Courts to to bare minimum. A member of the Bar is suppose to be friend of the court and ensures and help the court in providing justice to the litigants. But nowadays the lawyers acting on monetary considerations and often defy the solemn duty as a honourable member of this noble profession.

Shri S.M.N. Raina former justice of Madhya Pradesh High Court has narrated a very interesting episode in his book *Law, Judges and Justice (p. 148)* which was told to him by Shri Bishambhar Dayal former Chief Justice of M.P. High Court, which shows how dirty tricks are employed by some criminal lawyers in trial courts to secure acquittal. The episode is: "Once a person who had just committed murder approached a lawyer in his chamber and fell at his feet making a full confession of his crime and pleaded that he should be saved from the legal consequences. The lawyer thought over the matter, pacified him and asked him to sit down quietly. Then he asked his orderly to close down the chamber and he himself walked out. The orderly brought a baton and gave few blows with it on the person, so as to leave visible marks of injury including bleeding. The lawyer walked in after some time and told the accused that the injuries inflicted on him would save him from clutches of law. He asked him to go to the police station and immediately make a report that he was assaulted by the deceased and under an apprehension of death he had wielded his axe in order to defend himself. The accused was also told that if the police did not send him immediately for medical examination, he should go to a particular doctor and obtain a medical report for him and then come back to him." The case is an example of various methods adopted by lawyers to defend their clients and defeat justice.

It must, therefore, be realized that without the assistance of a competent and honest lawyer the task of the judge becomes extremely difficult and results into failure of justice.

□

(C) Role of Police and Other Agencies

The principle of natural justice lays that justice should not only be done but seem to be done. This is mainly to inspire confidence in the parties as well as people at large. In *Visakhapatnam Motor Transport* vs. *Bangaru* (AIR 1953 Madras 709); Chief Justice Rajamannar observed that it was an accepted principle that justice should not only be done but manifestly and undoubtedly seem to be done. I intend to quote the following observation of Chief Justice of Great Britain Lord Hewart.

"Nothing is to be done which creates even a suspicion that there has been an improper interference with the course of justice".

Another collar of the maxim is that a person cannot be both a suspect and approver. But in our judicial system the maxim is violated at the time of stage of investigation. Our police and other investigating agencies are supposed to investigate the matter and bring the facts before the judge to enable him to deliver the justice with the help of learned advocates. But it is very unfortunate that the police and investigation agencies want to convert the trial into conviction. During the course of investigation suspects are made as approver/prosecution witnesses and they save themselves from punishment of their wrong deeds by becoming prosecution witnesses/approvers. The officials of police/investigating agencies are rewarded on the basis of success of cases in prosecution. In other words, their promotion depends upon the conviction rate of the cases they handled. In Central Bureau of Investigation (CBI), the confidential reports of public prosecutors are written by the police officers which is the major hindrance in proper functioning of public prosecutors. Instead of helping the courts in arriving to a just decision, the public prosecutors with a sole objective of insuring the conviction of accused to please their bosses. It is true that distrust of police is a big handicap to the prosecution in bringing real offender to the book and getting him punished and sometimes an innocent person is held on the basis of false and fabricated evidence in order to show that the police is quite efficient.

Several times courts have passed strictures against the police. The modern scientific methods of investigation such as establishing the identity of the culprits by the means of finger prints are rarely used during investigation with the result they are tempted to fabricate evidence for securing a conviction of a person whom they believe to be guilty. Sometimes in an anxiety to resolve the mystery of a sensational case, even an innocent person is held guilty on the basis of false and fabricated evidences. In fact, the distrust of police is, therefore, a general feature of the administration of criminal justice in India.

On 13/12/2012, Shri Joginder Singh former Director of CBI disclosed on a T.V channel that during the investigation of Fodder Scam he was called by then Prime Minister Shri. I.K. Gujral and was asked to see about Shri Laloo Prasad Yadav. On the same day Shri. U.S. Sharma former Director of CBI admitted interference of senior officers in high profile cases. In case of 2G Spectrum Scam too CBI came into action only after Hon'ble Supreme Court took cognizance of 1.76 lakh crore Scam. In criminal justice investigation is very vital part of justice. An important and independent investigation can help the judge to reach to a just conclusion. Such type of interference of executive and bureaucracy will hamper the justice and only judges and judicial machinery cannot be blamed for falling credibility of our judicial system. CBI was established under Delhi Police Special Establishment Act to keep watch on corruption in Central Government and other organizations. But politicisation of CBI in recent times has questioned on the establishment of CBI. In my opinion all the investigation agencies should be kept out of the administrative control of executive to ensure justice to all.

□

(D) Role of Witnesses

A witness is very important chain in matter of criminal justice. A judge decides the case on the basis of material available on record. But it cannot take into consideration anything that is not on the records. In such things, he has to depend on oral evidences and in oral evidences the witness is very important. My experience says that in most of the cases witnesses are tutored by the lawyers. As per practice witnesses are sworn to tell the truth but they usually tell lies. Sometimes, it is amazing that even educated and well-placed persons resorting to falsehood. The amount of lies that is usually hurled at the courts is extremely depressing. Undoubtedly, it is the duty of the judge to find the truth from chaff of lies, but sometimes the efforts of judge may prove futile where the traces of truth are so inextricably mixed up with the falsehood that is difficult to separate the truth which may lead to failure of justice.

It is a common feature of our judicial system that witnesses are tutored to tell lies, when the tutoring is done by a layman the lies can be easily exposed in cross examination by a competent lawyer, but when a witness is trained to tell lies and mislead the court by an expert lawyer, it is very difficult to break the witnesses and expose the falsity of the witness and its testimony. The lies in the testimony of witness which is tutored by a competent and expert lawyer, acts like a guided missile to frustrate justice completely. It is very important for our judicial system that lawyers appearing in the trial courts should not be a party to the tutoring of witness as we have seen in famous BMW case. Anand. It must therefore be realized that without the assistance of a competent, efficient and honest lawyer and an honest witness the judge's task in reaching to the truth becomes extremely difficult and results in failure of justice and judge cannot be blamed for justice.

Justice S.M.N. Raina of M.P High Court narrates an incident in his book *Law, Judges and Justice* (P. 150) that "In a session trial before me the case of prosecution was that the deceased was assaulted mercilessly by Lathi in a broad day light at about 3 p.m. in a marketplace and there were about as many as seven eyewitnesses. Although these witnesses had fully supported the case of the prosecution in their statement to the police, yet they turned hostile in the court during trial. They admitted that they were there when the assault took place but they could not properly see and identify the assailant." Thus, all that was proved from evidence that the deceased was assaulted mercilessly and that he succumbed to his injuries at the spot but there was nothing to connect the accused with the crime.

Thus, it is believed that the witnesses have scant regard for truth as well as their oath. It is also a matter of common experience that in almost every criminal case in which an influential man is involved the witness turns hostile. If important witness turns hostile, the case may turn in acquittal even though the accused may be guilty.

The witnesses do not dare to speak against influential person and the results end with acquittal. To overcome this difficulty sometimes false witnesses are set up either by the relation of the victim or by the police. The criminal law in the country is grossly inadequate to bring the offenders to book and it can be a matter for high power committee to consider how it can be suitably modified without involving any risk of an innocent person being convicted.

Thus, the justice cannot be delivered only by the judges, justice can be delivered when all the functionaries of justice namely judges, lawyers, witness and the police work together honestly with full sincerity. In other words, these are four pillars on whose our judicial system runs. If any of the pillars will try to run away from discharging its duties, the system of justice would suffer. In fact, only judges are not accountable to judiciary rather other three are also equally accountable to judicial system.

□

(E) Role of Media in Criminal Justice

The media has a commitment to the basic human rights of accused persons in a country governed by rule of law. The manner in which certain sections of the media have covered politically important cases, particularly those monitored by the Supreme Court and High Courts, gives the impression that every politician accused of an offence deserves to be punished, trial or no trial, and should not be released on bail. As a result of indiscriminate media coverage of legal proceedings, public opinion started building up against the accused not only with respect to the charges which are yet to be tried, but also with respect to bail. Even after the discharge of most of the accused in the Jain Hawala case, the loss of reputation suffered by the accused leaders remains unsalvaged. It will remain an irreparable loss. Such opinion-building against the accused is not conducive to a fair trial consistent with basic human rights. The presumption of innocence itself is a basic human right-vide Art 11 of the Universal Declaration of Human Rights. The intention of the media is not to interfere with the course of justice or bring to bear public opinion assiduously built up by the media to affect decision-making in courts. The unintended effect of one-sided coverage without highlighting the basic human rights of accused persons is likely to interfere with the course of justice and result in miscarriage of justice. Strictly speaking, it is contempt of court to build up public opinion against accused persons in any criminal case. In the words of Lord Reid "anything in the nature of prejudgement of a case or of specific issues in it is objectionable not only because of its possible effect on that particular case but also because of its side effects which may be far-reaching. Responsible 'mass-media' will do their best to be fair, but there will also be ill-informed, slapdash or prejudiced attempts to influence the public. If people are led to think that it is easy to find the truth disrespect for the processes of the law could follow and, if mass media are allowed to judge, unpopular people and unpopular causes will fare very badly. Most cases of prejudging of issues fall within the existing authorities on contempt."

Media coverage of court proceedings is necessary. At the same time, it is the duty of the media to emphasise the pre-requisites of a fair trial and the basic human rights of accused persons including the right to bail pending investigation and trial. Media coverage should not be allowed unwittingly to become media intrusion in administration of justice. The criminal justice system remains the same irrespective of the nature of offence and the position of an accused. Such a system which assures a fair trial even to a person accused of the heinous offence of murder cannot deny the human rights to political leaders accused of economic offences. It is the duty of every institution and individual to uphold the human rights and facilitate their enforcement in any civilised society.

Justice R.S. Sarkaria in a speech delivered by him as the then Chairman, Press Council of India on World Freedom Day on May 3, 1994 at U.N. Information Centre, New Delhi, stated as follows: "It will not be out of place to mention here that it was disclosed at the International Conference held in Stockholm in June, 1991, that when the Swedish Prime Minister (Mr. Olfe Palme) was assassinated and the suspect was arrested and put on trial, the Swedish Press did not disclose the identity of the assailant before he was tried and convicted by the trial court. This is, one of the salutary norms of journalistic ethics which is being observed meticulously in Sweden though there is no law as such of contempt of court in that country."

"It is the function and right of the media to gather and convey information to the public and to comment on the administration of justice including cases before, during and after trial, without violating the presumption of innocence."

"The basic principle does not exclude the preservation by law of secrecy during the investigation of crime even where investigation forms part of the judicial process. Secrecy in such circumstances must be regarded as being mainly for the benefit of persons who are suspected or accused, to preserve the presumption of innocence."

Freedom of speech and expression itself is a basic human right, but not an absolute right. It is subject to reasonable restrictions. One such restriction is that it shall not be exercised in a manner so as to influence the mind of the judge in a pending case or so as to cause prejudice to the accused person. The right to a fair trial is basic to the rule of law. It is the duty of the media to respect this right and also appreciate that it is the duty of a judge to arrive at a correct decision in every case objectively uninfluenced by extraneous considerations. If media publicity becomes a factor reckon with for a judge or a court that will be the beginning of the end of the rule of law. The role of media in the O.J. Simpson trial is not an example worthy of emulation. Judges are human beings. After the advent of electronic media, the tendency to render populistic judgements or pass orders which would hit the headlines is, regrettably, on the increase. This is a disturbing trend. In this context the suggestion made by Justice P.B. Sawant, Chairman, Press Council that while reporting court news it would be better not to mention the names of judges in the media deserves serious consideration.

□

Judicial Reforms in Crime against Women

Crime against women is cause of concern for the entire society. On 1/12/2012, the incident of gang rape in the capital in a moving bus is the most shocking incident of a heinous sexual assault has stunned the nation. The 23-year-old women has become a symbol of crimes against women in the country and has forced a pained and anguished nation to seek answers. Though the issue of crime against women is too old, perhaps first time being openly discussed. Law and order, judicial reforms, punishment meted out to the offenders and patriarchal Indian mindsets are being addressed in public domain. Now the time has come to act. There are different segments of action to be taken to crush the crime against women.

1. Protection to women
2. Increase in case of reporting
3. Increase in conviction rate
4. Exemplanary Punishment
5. Settlement of Victims

First step needs to be taken by the state is to provide protection to the women at workplace and otherwise.

The police require to post more personnel specially in metropolitan cities. It should have better trained manpower and more women staff at stations and P.C.R's. Police patrolling should be increased at night. The women are frequently harassed at their workplace. The Supreme Court of India has issued guidelines in 1997 for protection of women from sexual harassment at workplace but the incidents of sexual harassment at workplace against women are still alarming. The Government needs to start fast track plans to install a web of CCTV cameras with face recognition. The roads should have proper lighting and vulnerable near shopping complexes and malls should be provided proper lighting and security arrangements. It is very unfortunate that the Central Government provides ₹ 3000 billion for social sector benefits and subsidies but spends only ₹ 10 billion on Security.

Large number of cases of crime against women are not reported by the victim. The treatment of the police as well as the society prevents the victims from reporting the incidents of crime against them. The lengthy procedure and unduly long time taken by the court is the main reason of women not coming to police to register the case of rape or molestation. Unfortunately, crime against women and their exploitation has multiplied marifolds in recent years in spite of laws to protect and safeguard their interest. This is evident from the fact that rape takes place one in every 29 minutes, sexual harassment in every 53 minutes, molestation in every 15 minutes, cruelty by husband or relatives in every nine minutes and dowry deaths every 77 minutes. The number of cases registered with the police are very less in comparison to the total number of case of crime against women.

The rate of conviction in case crime against women is more alarming. The rate of conviction in such cases is only 26.9%. The following figure shows the dismal rate of conviction in crime against women in year 2011.

There is a demand of death sentence by large section of the people and women organizations in particular in the wake of increasing cases of rape in the country. But the low rate of conviction does not make a case for capital punishment for people involved in rape cases. When the criminal is sure of getting exoneration, why should they fear from quantum of punishment?

On quantum of punishment, there are different parameters in different part of the world.

CRIMES AGAINST WOMEN IN 2011
(national figures, courtesy NCRB)

Crime	**Case Reported**	**Case conviction**
Rape*	24206	26.4%
Molestation	42968	27.7%
Sexual Harassment	8570	45.8%
Kidnapping & abduction	35565	28.1%
Cruelty by husband and relatives	99135	20.2%
Importation of girls	80	7.89%
Total crime against women	**228650**	**26.9%**

COUNTRY	LAW ABOUT RAPE	PUNISHMENT
1. India	A man is said to commit 'rape' has sexual intercourse with a woman against her will and without her consent.	Minimum seven years and Maximum sentence is life term.
2. U.K.	Rape Law is gender neutral, it includes Penile penetration without consent.	Maximum Sentence life term
3. U.S.A.	There is no national law. Each state has its own laws. In most states the definition of rape is broad with respect to genders and the nature of the acts involved.	Varies. Wisconsin for example has chemical castration and Texas has surgical castration.
4. China	The definition of rape is narrow. Rape law are not gender neutral. The offence includes raping of a woman by violence, coercion or any other means.	Death penalty
5. Iran	Convictions are made either by confession or judges' knowledge rather than witnesses.	Death penalty

It is evident from above information that England and India are the two countries where there is lighter punishment for rape crimes in comparison to U.S.A. China and Islamic countries including Iran. As a result in India and England the number of rape cases have increased considerably in recent years as is evident from the report of British Survey 2000 which estimated that one in twenty women had been raped since the age of 16 and one in ten had experienced some form of sexual assault (including rape).

□

Settlement of Victims

Three stories have been published in *Hindustan Times* dated 22/12/2012 regarding problems of raped victims faced by them after their victimization.

In the 1st story, the victim was a 16-year-old girl had gone to a stationary shop when she was dragged into another shop and was raped by four men on December 04, 2012. They threatened her not to approach the police as they had filmed the act and if she approaches the police they will make it public. So devastated was she that she was unable to narrate the incident to anyone including family at first but later confided to her mom. They went to the police station to get a complaint lodged. But the police refused to lodge a case, finally a case was registered on 4 December. Police insisted that she should visit the police station with which she was uncomfortable.

The accused were booked under various sections that attract lesser punishments. But her trauma did not end there, their relatives started trauming them and the entire family was forced to move out of the city. She is currently staying with a relative. She wants to study but could not muster the courage to go to the school.

In the second story, a 14-year-old was raped by her father over a year in his house in Sonia Vihar in East

Delhi. The mother of the victim died a few years ago. She was even restricted for her movement around the colony by the father. The girl had stopped leaving her home, one day she finally gathered the courage to inform the police. After the complaint the police arrested the accused and asked the welfare committee to move her to a shelter house as no relative is ready to take her.

After one year of being raped, she complained

14-year-old raped by dad, doesn't have a home now

The teenager was raped by her father for over a year, but she could not gather the courage to file a complaint. "When I did, I was shifted to a shelter home as I was afraid of entering that house again. With my father behind the bars, the police officials suggested that I should seek shelter in one of these homes," she said.

> "When I complained about my father, I was shifted to a shelter home as I was afraid of entering that house again. The police officials suggested that I seek seek shelter there."

The 14-year-old and her father used to live in their Sonia Vihar house in east Delhi after her mother died a few years ago. "I had never imagined that my father will rape me. He even restricted my movement around the colony," one day, she finally gathered the courage to inform the police.

After the complaint, police arrested the accused father and asked the Child Welfare Committee (CWC) to move her to a shelter house.

"The decision was taken to make sure that the girl felt safe and was able to continue her studies. Her father ruined her life but we are now trying to bring back normalcy in her life" a senior police officer said.

However, the CWC is of the opinion that if the girl is willing to live with a relative, she would be allowed to leave. "She has already gone through a lot and needs her loved ones around. If her relatives are ready to take her in,

She hasn't been paid wages for 3 months

22-year-old raped, so fiancé deserted her

On March 15 this year, the 22-year-old resident of Mangolpuri got a call from her neighbour and acquaintance. He asked her to reach his house as his "mother wanted to meet" her.

When she got there, he was sitting alone in the house. He locked the doors, sedated and raped her. "He beat me up badly and my neck hurt for days when I tried to defend myself," she recalled.

For days, the fear of being ostracised kept her quiet, but later she confided in her sister who got a case registered.

Eight months later, the 22-year-old from Assam is unable to forget anything. "Everything has changed. My landlord wants me to leave the house and I have to constantly fight with him. At my workplace, people treat me differently," she said. In fact, the shoe factory where she works has not paid her for three months now.

> "Everything has changed now. My landlord wants me to leave the house and I have to constantly fight with him. At my workplace, people treat my differently."

Right now, her biggest concern is getting married. The man who had promised to marry her has changed his mind. He even took away her belongings. "I want to get married and lead a happy life but it is becoming difficult for me to sustain myself," she said.

She had come to Delhi a year ago for a job. After landing in Delhi, she lived with her sister for some time but now lives alone in Mangolpuri. "He is behind bars but I am still socially ostracised. I don't know whom to ask for help," she said.

HTC

She wanted to study, but didn't have courage

16-year-old rape victim forced to leave home

On December 4, the 16-year-old girl had gone to a stationary shop in the market near her home when she was dragged into another shop. Four men then raped her. "They threatened me that they had filmed the act and if I approached the police, they will make it public," the girl told HT.

So devastated was she that she was unable to narrate the incident to anyone in the family at first, but later confided in her mom. She also alleged that two days later, they went to the police station to get a complaint lodged. But the police refused to lodge a case. Finally, the case was registered

insisted that I visit the police station, with which I was uncomfortable," the 16-year-old said.

> "I was standing at a shop when I was dragged into the one next to it. Four men raped me. They said they had filmed the act and will make it public if I approached the police."

The accused were booked under various sections that attract lesser punishment. But her trauma did not end here. "Our relatives started taunting us. We had no option but to move her out of the city. She is currently staying with a relative. She wants to study, but could not muster the courage to go to school. She is the victim, and yet she's been punished," the victim's brother said.

The family is also planning to leave the neighbourhood as they have been boycotted socially. "At one point, I even contemplated committing suicide. But looking at my sister, I decided to fight the battle. We will not

MAN GETS 8-YR IMPRISONMENT FOR RAPING DAUGHTER

Sumit Saxena
■ sumit.saxena@hindustantimes.com

NEW DELHI: A 22-year-old law student won a legal battle against her father, who had raped and assaulted her since she was 13. The woman is a resident of Pitampura in northwest Delhi. The victim had mustered courage to fight back in 2008. Her grandmother helped her file an FIR against her father.

Last week, a Delhi court convicted the victim's father and sentenced him to eight years' imprisonment. Additional sessions judge Yashwant Kumar supported his verdict with the victim and her grandmother's statement. The doctor's testimony too corroborated the girl's statement. The victim's mother, who faced abetment charges, was acquitted for lack of evidence.

Dinesh Sharma (name changed) was arrested but was released on bail.

The victim registered a complaint of physical assault against her father at the age of 17. During her medical examination, the doctors observed that she was subjected to extreme sexual activity.

The victim told the police that her mother used to administer some liquid, which made her unconscious and then her father would rape her.

During his arguments, public prosecutor Atul Srivastav contended that as the accused was the father, he should be sentenced for life.

THE VICTIM TOLD THE POLICE THAT HER MOTHER WOULD ADMINISTER SOME LIQUID AND HER FATHER WOULD RAPE HER

In the third story published by *Hindustan Times* a 22-year-old resident of Mangolpuri got a call from her neighbor and acquaintance. He asked her to reach his house as his mother wants to meet her. When she got there, he locked the doors sedated and raped her and she was beaten by the accused badly, for days the fear of being ostracized kept her quiet but later confided to her sister who got a case registered. For the victim everything has changed her landlord wants to change the house and at her workplace people treat her differently. In fact, the shoe factory where she works has not paid her for three months. The man who has promised her to marry has changed his mind.

In another story published on 24December 2012, a 22-year-old law student won a legal battle against her father, who had raped and assaulted since she was 13. The victim has mustered a courage to fight back in 2008, her grandmother helped to file a FIR against her father. A Delhi court convicted her father and sentenced him to eight years of imprisonment. During the argument, the public prosecutor requested the court that accused was the father of the victim and a rape by the father of her own daughter is the ghastliest action on the earth and he should at least be given the sentence of life. But the court has taken a lenient view in the case. On the basis of these four cases the settlement of victims and quantum of punishment are the two basic questions which require to be sorted out in rape cases. The attitude of the society changes towards the rape victim and it should be the prime duty of the state to provide shelter to the victim just after the lodging the F.I.R and the quantum of punishment should be exemplanary in all the cases of crime against women. In cases where the accused is the closed relative of the victim, the minimum sentence should be life imprisonment with no facility of review of sentence or remittance of sentence.

Crime against women has to be waged by adopting a multiple approach and involving various sections of the society through systematic campaigns and various awareness programmes. Special support along with the legal protection, safeguards cooperation by the investigating agencies and people in prosecuting the criminals and desired reforms in criminal judicial system, including judges' sympathetic attitude towards victims of sexual assault are necessary to eradicate crime against women.

□

Suggestions for Streamlining Rape Laws

1. The delay in disposal of rape cases, which at present ranges between four to six, years be reduced. In this regard the trial case of Bilti Hota Mohanti of 2006, in which a German girl was raped, was decided in just nine days is a glaring example of speedy justice. In the impugned case Judge R.K. Maheswari of a fast track court in Alwar packed off Bilti Hota Mohanti, a 23-year-old computer engineer for raping the girl on March 2006, in a hotel, for seven years imprisonment and a fine of ₹ 10,000. The case shows that the delay in cases of crime against women can be reduced to a great extent.
2. Proper counseling should be provided to rape victims to inculcate confidence in them and initiate action immediately without delay.
3. A women's complaint that she has been raped must be taken as a face value in a conservative society like India where indelible stigma is attached to the victim and of course laws are extremely inadequate and need drastic changes.

4. The government should take up a package of measures including a network to prevent the loss of vital forensic evidence in rape cases and the requirement for a specialist second opinion before a decision is taken to initiate a rape prosecution as in the United Kingdom. This will ensure maximum conviction.
5. There is no specific provision in the Indian Penal Code to deal effectively the cases of child sex abuse. As a result many a time a culprit goes unpunished.

As stated by the Supreme Court of Canada that—

"If the criminal justice system is to effectively perform its role in determining and punishing Child Sexual Abuse, it is vital that the law provides a workable and decent and dignified means for the victim to tell her story in the court."

In addition to strengthening the law, it is necessary to have a cooperative victim professional investigation, diligent prosecution, expeditious trial and sensitive judges to ensure proper investigation, trial and conviction. In the sentencing, the courts are expected to consider all relevant facts and circumstances bearing on the question of sentence and proceed to impose a sentence which is commensurate with the gravity of a offence.

"Why Change in Law on Sexual Offences is Necessary"

The public outrage in the wake of the Delhi gang rape has been as much a reaction to the brutality of the case, as it has been against the pervasiveness of sexual violence in our society. Instead of condemnation and action, rape cases frequently evoke public statements blaming the victims, and calls to reign in women's freedom. That our social structures and mindsets remain patriarchal is well known. The question however is, to what extent does the law counter societal misogyny in the way it frames and responds to sexual violence? Do the criminal laws establish norms that uphold women's bodily integrity and dignity in all situations, against all offenders without selectivity or discrimination?

Crafted in the nineteenth century to protect purity of male lineage, rather than women's bodily integrity, the Indian Penal Code continues to be steadfast to its patriarchal moorings. It treats non-consensual peno-vaginal penetration as the only serious sexual offence under sections 375 and 376. Marital rape is expressly de-criminalised. Other non-consensual penetrative sexual acts such as insertion of the finger or objects into the vagina, anus or mouth of the woman are not included within the scope of rape. Instead they are subsumed under Section 377 that pertains to 'carnal intercourse', which unlike procreative intercourse, is described as being 'against the order of nature'. Historically, this provision has served to criminalise homosexuality.

Consent is not used consistently in law to distinguish sexual wrongs from sexual rights. The de-criminalisation of marital rape is not the only means by which the wife's status as the husband's property is legally secured. Adultery provision (section 497) criminalises consensual sex by the wife outside marriage, even as it excludes the husband's extra marital sex from the purview of criminality. The inconsistent approach to consent is also evident in the offences 'against the order of nature', which make no distinction between consensual and non-consensual sex. This subjective use of the term consent serves to uphold patrilineality and heteronomitivity in the law, rather than sexual autonomy and bodily integrity of women. The selective and subjective reading of consent spills beyond the statute to the judicial attitudes and the manner in which the courts appreciate evidence. A woman's conduct, clothes, references to old hymen tears and previous sexual history have been the basis for acquittals, and often, for reducing a rape sentence to 2 to 3 years, when the statutory minimum is 7 years in the law. Studies show that rape prosecutions, from reporting, investigation, medical procedures, cross examination and judicial reasoning are demeaning and hostile to women.

All non-penetrative sexual assault, which constitutes the widest swathe of offences against women, are collapsed under 'outraging the modesty' of a woman under section 354. Regardless of the gravity of the assault, and its repercussions on women, the provision provides only a maximum sentence of 2 years. This provision is invoked for a range of non-penetrative sexual assault, from lesser to grave, such as public disrobing and parading of women, tonsuring the woman's hair, groping - all of which have been trivialized. The mob molestation, groping and public stripping of a young woman in Guwahati in July 2012, was revealing for more than one reason first, it highlighted public apathy towards a grotesque spectacle of violence as it played out on a busy street in the centre of the state capital; and second, because the police failed to take any action until several days later, following national outrage.

The lack of recognition to a large spectrum of harassment and intimidation such as stalking and voyeurism is a serious shortcoming in the law. Failure to name, recognise and punish each of these offences in the law creates the impunity for wide ranging sex crimes, encouraging offenders to graduate from lesser to more serious offences without fear of legal consequences.

It is in this context that the report of the three member committee headed by Justice Verma (JVC report) assumes significance for women's equality and gender justice. The recommendations introduce a paradigm shift in the way sexual violence against women is framed. After 64 years of the Indian republic, women's security concerns have for the first time have been framed within the constitutional concepts of equality and non-discrimination. The recommendations make bodily security, integrity and sexual autonomy for women central, rejecting patriarchal references of protectionism and modesty. The women's movement has been campaigning for reform of laws relating to sexual violence for two decades, without much success. The JVC report, proposes comprehensive reforms, framed to recognise the bodily security and integrity of women in all situations and against all perpetrators without discrimination, or reference to public morality. These recommendations are a step towards fulfillment of the constitutional values of sex and gender equality that must be implemented at the earliest.

Justice J. S. Verma Committee report and Ordinance—

In view of the incident of brutal gang rape in Delhi on 16 December 2012 a committee under the chairmanship of Justice J.S. Verma was set up and on the recommendation of committee's recommendation. Government of India has promulgated on ordinance. The ordinance has also been given the consent by the President. The new law has accepted Justice Verma committee's recommendations to treat voyeurism, stalking, disrobing of women and acid attacks on specific offenders under the Indian Penal Code. The change will raise eveteasing from being considered a minor offence to a serious crime attracting enhanced punishment. The recommendation to raise the maximum punishment for rape from existing 10 years to life term has been accepted. For repeat offenders the life imprisonment will cover his entire life and not Just 14 years as in the case now. The rape has been made gender neutral and the word rape has been replaced by the expression sexual assault. The ordinance has rejected rightly the recommendation of inclusion of marital rape as an offence including forced sex in a period of separation.

The committee submitted its 630 pages report to the Government on 23rd January 2013. The committee received 80,000 suggestions from various law known personalities, women organizations and social activists.

The Committee Has Recommended-

Enhancing punishment upto 20 years imprisonment for rape and murder and life for gang rape but refrained from suggesting death penalty. It suggested amendment of criminal laws to provide for higher punishment to rapist including those belonging to police and public servants. Justice Verma said "we have not recommended death penalty as we had overwhelming suggestions against it. The women groups unanimously were against it and that is why we thought that it is a strong reason to respect that view particularly in view of the modern trend also". He said that the failure of governance was the root cause of crime against women. He also said it was equally shocking that there was total apathy of everyone who had a duty to perform. Complimenting the youth for their mature response, Mr. Verma said "Youth has taught us what we, the older generation, were not aware of. I was struck by the peaceful manner in which the protests were carried out...the youth rose to the occasion."

Highlights—

- Enhancing punishment of upto 20 years imprisonment for rape and murder and life for gang rape. The present law provides for punishment of imprisonment ranging from 7 years to life.
- Rejects chemical castration and death for rapists.
- Politicians should be ineligible to contest if court has taken cognizance of crime.
- Observation homes for juvenile offenders should be run in a manner which is in the spirit of Juvenile Justice Act.
- Establish a new constitutional authority like CAG for education and non-discrimination of women and children so that there is a proper audit of laws.
- Government must tackle trafficking of children and maintain data on the same.
- New offences have been created including disrobing a woman, voyeurism, stalking & trafficking.

- Introduced a heinous crime offence of "trafficking of a person" punishable with imprisonment from 7 years to life sentence.
- Introduced the heinous offence of acid attack.
- Intentional touching will constitute the offence of sexual assault for which punishment will be a maximum of 5 years rigorous imprisonment or fine or both
- Use of words, gesture which create an unwelcome threat of sexual nature or advance would invite a maximum punishment of one year imprisonment or fine or both.
- Change in Section 100 of Indian Penal Code (IPC) dealing with right of private defence which extends to causing death.
- Replacement of Section 375 defining rape by defining unnatural acts.p
- Need to retake into continuance o Armed Forces Special Powers Act (AFSPA).
- Increase the strength of judges without affecting the quality.
- Implement police reforms for better autonomy and functioning of police force.
- Government must ensure that law enforcement agencies do not become tools at the hands of political masters. Bring transparency and accountability to the functioning of all institutions of governance.
- The ambiguity on who is responsible for the law & order issue in Delhi should be removed with immediate effect. All marriages should be registered. Any officer who fails to report a case of

rape or delays the same should be punished. No need for sanction to prosecute force member involved in sexual crimes. Rape victim should not be cross questioned on moral character. Framed a protocol for medical examination of rape victim. Special Commissioners should be appointed to address the issues of violence against women in conflict areas such as Jammu & Kashmir, Chattisgarh & Manipur.

□

Judicial Independency and Super-Session of Judges

Independence of judiciary is very vital in democratic system, but it does not mean a license to discharge the judicial function in whatever manner one pleases. It calls for a judicial discipline governing the discharge of judicial function in a purposeful manner. Judicial independence merely consists in giving a decision without fear or favor without malice or ill, will. It should not give rise to judicial arrogance on account of an assumed air of superiority over other organs of the state. The three organs of the state, namely the Legislature, the Executive and the Judiciary are of equal importance of its own in its own sphere. They are supplementary to one another within the framework laid down by the Constitution rather competing centers of power. There should be complete harmony between these organs and each must function with due sense of respect and consideration for others.

But the independence of judiciary came under a severe test when Smt. Indira Gandhi was Prime Minister. In 1973 Shri. A.N. Roy was appointed Chief Justice of India by superseding three fellow judges, namely Justice Sheetal, Justice Hedge and Justice Grover who were senior to him. The government took this stand because in fundamental rights case these judges expressed view regarding the interpretation of the Constitution which was not palatable to the government. The judgment in fundamental rights case was delivered on 24/04/1973 and these judges expressed the view that Parliament cannot amend the Constitution so as to destroy or damage any of essential features of the Constitution. The government was taking unusual interest in the case and wanted the Supreme Court to concede to the Parliament Plenary power to amend the Constitution. For this purpose a threat of political action was given in the court as it reveals from the observation of Palkhivala: "During the hearing of the fundamental rights case the Attorney General appearing for the Union of India and the counsel for some states expressly referred in open court, both orally and in writing, to the alternative of political action, if the Supreme Court ruling did not find favor with the government. This background is not without significance in considering the causes of supercession."

The view expressed by these three judges was resented by the Government and on 25 April,1973 just after two days of the judgment Shri. A.N. Roy who was junior to them was appointed Chief Justice of India. On the same evening Supreme Court Bar Association met to consider government's action. Moving the resolution Shri. M.C. Chagla former Chief Justice of Bombay High Court observed "Today is the blackest day in the administration of justice. Something which we all admired in our life and the principles for which we stood are fast disappearing". Former Chief Justice M. Hidaytullah explained the consequences of super cession in the following terms:

"Today the whole of judiciary is suspect because it is not accepted in some quarters that some judge would want to trim his opinion so as to be able to get on. So that judges as I said would want to look forward to something coming to them and therefore modulate their decision to the exigencies of their situation and not to the situation of the country and the court".

Justice Hedge observed in his book *Crisis in Indian Judiciary* (p. 48) "The action of the Government has shattered the confidence of the people in judiciary. Its image stands tarnished. A major blow has been struck to independence of judiciary. The government's action was pre-meditated and calculated. Evidently, the Government intended to strike terror into the heart of judiciary throughout the country. Judges both in High Court and Supreme Courts have been told in unmistakable terms to behave or get superseded." As observed by M.C. Setalvad, hereafter—"Every judge of the Supreme Court when making a decision in which government policy is in question will have to think of his prospects of being appointed the Chief Justice of India and bear in mind what the philosophy of the government of the day is, if he wants to be good with the government in order to earn his appointment as the Chief Justice. Take the judges of the High Court. Naturally and rightly they all aspire, as soon as they grow senior, to be selected for the highest court in the land. But they must bear in mind that in order to be selected they must also interpret the constitution, not as they think it requires to be interpreted, but according to the philosophy of the government in power at the Centre for the time being".

Shri. N.A. Palkhiwala regretted the supersession in the following terms—"Anxiety to get a preferment or promotion is a human weakness and many may fall a prey to the temptation. The citizens of their country have already lost several valuable rights as a result of the various amendments to the constitution, but that loss is small, compared with what they lost, as a result of the denigration of the judiciary. As mentioned by several eminent jurists and lawyers, today judiciary is suspect. Its most honest decision in favor of the government is likely to be viewed with suspicion. Even with best of efforts, it is bound to take a long time to rehabilitate the judiciary".

Contrarily Shri. Gokhale then Law Minister strongly supported the government view that it was open to the government to appoint a person as Chief Justice whose philosophy was acceptable to it. He also quoted the following words of Pandit Jawaharlal Nehru as Prime Minister in 1949 while speaking in the Constituent Assembly—

"No Supreme Court and no judiciary can stand in judgment over the sovereign will of Parliament representing the will of the entire community. If we go wrong here and there, it can point it out, but in the ultimate analysis, where the future of the community is concerned, no judiciary can come in the way and if it comes in the way, ultimately the whole constitution is a CREATURE of Parliament...it is obvious that no court, no system of judiciary can function in the nature of a third House, as a kind of third house of correction".

One thing that is to be kept in mind that a judge of a high caliber and integrity should not be denied his promotion merely because his judgments are not favorable to the Government. Further to safeguard the Constitution in the duty of the judiciary and the judiciary should not be forced to give up.

□

Judicial Reforms—Now Necessary: Some Suggestions

Inadequacies of our judicial system which is resulting into its expending failure in delivering justice, our judicial system badly requires judicial reform. In words of Shri. Palkhiwala our laws and their interpretation and adjudication led to enormous misery for the litigants and forced people to look for extra-legal alternatives. A house owner even finds impossible to evict a tenant even for self occupation with the help of court and are forced to adapt out of court settlements. In the process of achieving goals by extra legal alternate methods, a new industry of administering readymade justice by using strong arm tactics has been set up by local hoodlums in almost all of our cities and towns and even in rural areas. In the criminal matters from the stage of FIR to the trial these hoodlums along with some bureaucrats, leaders, police officers manipulate the things in favor of culprits.

The failure of the civil and criminal justice system is because of abnormal delays in litigation and huge pendency in courts. It is estimated that approximately 38 million cases are pending in different courts all over the country. About 20 million cases are pending in District Courts, High Courts and Supreme Court and about 18 million cases are pending in lower courts. Even the cases involving extremely grave offences with direct impact on public order and national security there are abnormal delays. These are harrowing tales of innocent citizens accused of petty offences languishing in jails as under trials for decades most often the time spent in prison during trial exceeds the maximum punishment permissible under law.

As per an estimation, India has only about 11 judges per million population which is the lowest ratio in the world. The cases pending exceed about 30 thousand per million population. The delays, the complexity and the unending appeals make litigation very expensive and such costs is beyond the reach of most of the citizens.

The failure of criminal justice system has led to the near break down of public order in many parts of the country. The arbitrary and unaccountable functioning of the police has led to complete alienation of citizens from the state. Complete politicalization of police force has led to lack of impartiality in investigation. In recent times, it has been observed that elected governments are abusing their powers by closing serious criminal charges against their supporters and foist false cases against their opponents. This alarming situation calls for speedy remedial measures. The judicial reforms should be capable of providing speedy and efficient justice to ordinary people. Several Law Commission reports have made out a case for many specific judicial reforms but unfortunately very little has been done in this area and resulting into failure of judicial system. The following are some of major reforms that need to be taken care of without further delay—

1. Increase Judge-Population Ratio

As stated the judge-population ratio in India is lowest in the world. The number of judges in our country is approximately 11 per million population. In higher judiciary large number of judges sit as constitutional courts everyday with the power of interpreting constitution and quashing laws on the ground that they are unconstitutional whereas in U.S.A. the Supreme Court alone sits as constitutional bench and other Federal Courts have limited power to interpret the constitution. In India in spite of large number of judges in High Courts the ordinary people are not getting relief because of the reason that the judges are busy with constitutional matters and writs and appellant jurisdiction of High Courts is the area which is most neglected. At present what is needed is a substantial increase in the number of judges at the local level giving access to the ordinary people.

2. Creation of Indian Judicial Service

Transparency in judicial appointments have been caused of controversy in recent past. The efficiency is another requirement for ensuring a speedy and a just decision. In Subordinate courts, there have been inordinate delays and varying levels of efficiency. The Indian Judicial Service should be created as an All India Service under Article 132 of the Constitution. All the offices of the level of District and Sessions Judges should be held by person recruited through Indian Judicial Service after adequate training and exposure. Only such a meritocratic service with a competitive recruitment, high quality uniformal training and assured standard of probity and efficiency would be able to insure speedy justice which will be accessible to ordinary people. A fair proportion of the High Court judges could be drawn from the Indian Judicial Service.

3. Establishment of *Gram Nyayalaya*

Law Commission in its 114th report advocated for *Gram Nyayalaya*. To avoid long pendency of civil matters, rural courts with special magistrate should be formed having jurisdiction over a town or a part of town or group of villages. These magistrates should be appointed by district judges for a period of three to five years. They should have exclusive civil and criminal jurisdiction in small matters such as all civil disputes up to ` 1 lakh and criminal matters up to imprisonment of one year. Further certain civil disputes arising out of agrarian reforms, property disputes, family disputes and other matters as recommended by the Law Commission should be entrusted to these rural courts. In civil cases, there should be provision of revision by District Judge on grounds of improper application of law. In criminal matters where the imprisonment has been awarded there could be a provision for appeal to the Session Judge. The procedure in the *Gram Nyayalaya* should be simple and these courts should be duty bound to deliver the verdict within a period of 90 days. These *Gram Nyayalayas* will be of immense help on clearing the backlog of petty matters waiting in subordinate courts for disposal over a decade's period.

4. Appointment of a Judicial Commission

The present system of appointment of judges of higher judiciary lacks transparency and has become very dilatory and ineffective. The Supreme Court's efforts in arrogating to itself the complete power of appointment of judges made the situation worse. Shri. Arun Jaitly former Law Minister and Leader of Opposition in Rajya Sabha said that there are two kinds of judges—one who knows the law and the other who knows the law minister. His observation shows that all is not going well in collegium which appoints judges for the higher judiciary. It is absurd to assume that in a democratic society any organ of state should perpetuate without any degree of accountability to the people and the country. Justice Ramaswamy's impeachment case has amply proved that our Parliament has lost the power and will to act as a court in such impeachment trials. If a judge is appointed solely on the recommendation of judiciary and no judge can be impeached in practice, no matter how his conduct is or law inefficient his functioning is. Such situation can lead to judicial terrorism and result in unmitigated disaster to the governance process and society. So it is high time which requires appointment of judicial commission with members drawn from judiciary. The executive and the legislative and their recommendation is made binding on the President in all appointments of higher judiciary. Similarly, the judicial commission should be empowered to try errant judge and the President should be empowered, to remove the judge held guilty of high crimes and misdemeanors, on the recommendation of Judicial Commission.

5. Restriction on High Courts

The High Courts in India are overburdened with the pendency of backlog. Over 20 million cases are pending in higher judiciary. The writ jurisdiction which has now become all incompassive should be strictly forced on Rights to Life, Liberty and Equality before law. The creative expansion of writ jurisdiction that has now become the order of the day should be firmly curbed. Wherever the writ is applicable, the courts should have complete and unfettered powers to enforce their directives.

The High Court should not have the powers to interpret the Constitution except in matters involving state legislations. The interpretation of the Constitution should be done by the Supreme Court. In fact, the Supreme Court should function only as a constitutional court and a federal court. The matters relating to taxation, disciplinary action against employees and labour disputes should be kept beyond the purview of ordinary courts. They should be entrusted to the special tribunals with no provisions for appeal to higher courts except on the ground of interpretation of the Cconstitution.

6. Review of Judicial Procedures

Actually, the civil procedure and criminal procedure codes and the laws of evidence have become cumbersome, dilatory and often counterproductive. As such these procedural laws have to be modified to meet the requirement of modern judicial administration. In all trial courts, local language should be the only language to be used. Time limits should be prescribed for adjudication. The stays of proceeding and adjournment on one or the other pleas should be restricted. The right to get justice within one year in a criminal case and two years in a civil case should be constitutionally guaranteed. All the procedural laws should be suitably amended to ensure that the constitutional right to get justice within stipulated period can be enforced. There should be limitation of appeal such as only one appeal of review should be allowed in civil cases. The appeal should be disposed of within six months in a criminal case and within one year in a civil case. All stays should be prohibited except in exceptional circumstances for reasons specifically recorded in writing and no stays should be granted beyond a period of two weeks.

The time has now come when concerted efforts should be made to make our judicial system efficient, effective, fear less without affecting the functions of other organs of the state.

7. Establishment of Special Crime Investigation Police

In our country, the police performs multiple functions like law and order, crime investigation, intelligence gathering, riot control, security of state properties, protection of VIPs and traffic control. All in a single police is resulting into total collapse of criminal judicial system, because overburdened does not and cannot do justice with matters of investigation of criminal matters. The police force have become inefficient and far from impartiality. The government has taken complete powers of control over the crime investigation machinery as well as over legal authority. As a result criminal charges against the persons are dropped. In actual sense crime investigation has become a thing of partisan politics. It is therefore suggested for creation of an independent wing of police force to look after crime investigation which will work under the direct control of an independent prosecutor which should be a constitutional body. The court should held the prosecutor and the crime investigation police force accountable in their overall functioning. There can be fairness and justice to the common people of the country when the crime investigation is separated from the clutches of power politics. When the crime investigation machinery is directly accountable to the judiciary, the practice of torture, third degree method and extra-judicial execution and fake encounters will be stopped.

8. Unnecessary Detention should be Avoided

Unnecessary detention, under trial prisoners constitute bulk of India's prison population. Justice Mullah Committee[28] on jail reforms recorded that while the total prison population in India has shown a declining trend over the past few years, the rate of under trial prisoners per hundred of convicted persons went up to 149 as on 31/12/1980 and 160 as on 30 June 1981. The Seventh Finance Commission found that this ratio was very high in states like Assam, Bihar, Orissa, Uttar Pradesh and West Bengal. In some states it rose to 80% of the total inmate population. A report reveals that in Tihar Jail there are 900 to 1000 inmates against the total capacity of 3300 prisoners. In the context it needs to emphasize that the numbers of 90% of the total inmates are under trials and the position is going to get worse in the near future if the problem is not sorted out. Though Delhi High Court has recently issued an order to initiate immediate measures to decongest the Tihar Jail. Further right to speedy justice is a part of Article 21 of the Constitution, which stipulates right to life with dignity. Thus, the denial of justice, within a reasonable time, can tantamount to infringement of fundamental and if this trend continues our judicial system would be accused of making a mockery of the fundamental rights. As regards the effect of the overcrowding in prison, All India Jail Manual Committee of 1957-59 reported that "owing to continuous state of overcrowding, minimum standard for housing and equipment, sanitary service, water supply segregation of inmates of various categories, etc. cannot be properly maintained; unemployment and idleness increase in prisons; discipline become a complicated problem. Welfare and training of inmates becomes a difficult preposition. The overall efficiency of an institution thus gets lowered".

On the basis of foregoing facts, it is very necessary to adopt judicial reforms suggested above to ensure justice to common people of India.

□

Conclusion

In our country, justice is inaccessible to the common people in the present set up of judicial system. Today justice can be accessed through lawyers who are unaffordable to the common people. The delay and lethargy of our judicial system made justice a distant dream. In our system both the bar and the bench are supposed to be above law as 97% complaints against lawyers and 99% complaints against judges are dismissed. Less than 2% of the complaint are put on trial without any result or consequences. In such a situation, the Judicial Standard and Accountability Bill, 2010 is a ray of hope for common citizen of this country which is the largest democracy of the world and in a democracy all organ of the state are responsible and accountable to the people at large and judiciary is no exception. It is necessary for our judges to set an example and provide role models worth emulation. But we can proceed on the assumption that judges do no wrong as we assume about the king of British democracy. Therefore, in our society we require a system with the provision of checks and balances to restrain the misuse of power. In today, society, it is observed that the judges of the superior courts intent to take greater claim to immunity.

Undoubtedly, the number of judges involved in misconduct or corruption are very less but it is very painful to witness such eminent people involved in corruption. The judicial institution which are bestowed with a divine function needs to adopt a zero tolerance policy for such cases. Judges need to introspect and respect the collective judgement of the people of the country which expect accountability in our system.

The seat of justice in India has motto of *Satyamev jayate* meaning thereby let there be victory of truth or let the truth prevail. So it is expected that the seat of justice should prove to be the seat of god, at least to uphold to maintain truth and thereby dignity of the court.

With regard to transparency in appointment of judges there ought to be greater transparency, wider consultation and above all a fair consideration. It has also become equally important to place a great emphasis on integrity and an absolute impeccable character along with learning while selecting person for higher judiciary.

The concept of accountability involves not only the method of appointment but also the method of removal for deviant behavior. The only method of removal of judges is impeachment which has lost its sanctity due to political reasons as we have seen in case of Justice V. Ramaswami. It is high time we evolve a mechanism to keep a check on deviant behavior of judges.

The issue of large number of pending cases is undoubtedly an appalling problem. As we already know that justice delayed is justice denied. Though the quality of judicial functioning should not be compromised, yet some methods should be adopted to curb the large number of pending cases.

It must however be said appointment of competent person with undoubted integrity is the best way of controlling the inflow and expediting the disposal of cases.

The third point of consideration is the judicial activism which is also responsible for long arrears of pending cases in the High Court and Supreme Court. The most of the time of the judges are spend on disposal of writs and PIL on administrative matters and regular matters suffer and result into backlog of cases.

In conclusion, it is wrong to say that judiciary is not accountable or that it exercises power without accountability but it is because of a defective constitutional judicial system prevailing in India. Though entire responsibility of the situation cannot be put on our constitutional judicial system. Our elected body or executive on some occasion act irresponsibly for which a non-elected judiciary was provided as a check. The other organ like media and public opinion has not served the purpose. The judiciary in India enjoyed immense public confidence but the high expectation demand a proof of its utility and therefore the immense faith of people in our judiciary is today at the verge of collapse.

There is an urgent need to make empirical studies to various issue raised in the research work and take remedial steps to device ways and means to rectify the noted shortcomings of our judicial system. The task is difficult and daunting but by no mean impossible.

Today judiciary is required to function at a time when the country is passing through a drastic social and economic change caused by economic globalization, scientific and technological revolution. Hence, the law as well as courts must be instrumental in performing its role with much faster pace and as per expectation of the people of the country. I conclude with following saying that those who advocate justice must do justice. Judges are the instrument but justice is the end and judges have to accept the maxim, be you ever so high, the law is above you.

□

Bibliography

Books

1. S.P. Verma, *Indian Judicial System : Need and Direction of Reforms*, Kanishka Publishers (2004).
2. B.R. Sharma, *Judiciary on Trial*, Deep and Deep Publications (1989).
3. K. Mahesh and Bishwajit Bhattacharya, *Judging the Judges*, Gyan Publication House (1999).
4. S.M.N. Raina, *Law, Judges and Justice*, Vedpal Law House.

Articles

1. Prashant Bhushan, "Judicial Accountability or Illusion", *Economic and Political Weekly*, November 2006.
2. Arti Puri, "The Judges (inquiry) Bill 2006 vis-à-vis Accountability of Higher Judiciary in India', *MDU Law Journal* 12(2). 2007.
3. Prashant Bhushan, "Judicial Accountability: Asset Disclosure and Beyond", *Economic and Political Weekly*, September 12, 2009.
4. T.P. Kelu, "For whom the Judge is Born", 2009 (1), *Kerela law times*.

5. K. Ravinder Reddy, "Indian Judiciary and Accountability", *Andhra Law Times*. 2004 (7).
6. Amit A. Pai, "Judicial accountability—A Constitutional Analysis", *Madras Law Journal*, 2009. (8)
7. A.R. Lakshmanan, "Judicial accountability and legal reforms", 2009 (7), *Madras Law Journal*.
8. B. Padmanabha Holia, "Judicial accountability and transperancy in judgement", *AIR* 1998 (March)(86), 55".
9. Sunil V. Manohar, "The judicial (enquiry) bill 2006 : A remedy worse than the disease", *AIR* 2007 (Feb) 19.

Newspapers

1. Hindustan Times
2. Times of India
3. The Hindu
4. Indian Express.

Miscellaneous

1. Law Commission Reports
2. All India Reporter
3. Supreme Court Cases.

□

Endnotes

1. B.R. Sharma, *Judiciary on Trial: Appointment, Transfer, Accountability*, Deep and Deep Publications (1989).
2. Sir Jadunath Sarkar, 'Mughal Administration', M. C. Sarkar publisher, 29 (1935).
3. M.B. Ahmad, *Administration of Justice in Medieval India*, p. 55.
4. M.P. Jain, *Outline of Indian Legal History,* 2nd edition. 145-269 (1972).
5. Section 2, Indian High Court Act, 1861.
6. Granville Austin, *Indian Constitution : Corner Stone of Nation*, p. 170. (1966).
7. S.P. Verma, *Indian Judicial System: Need and Direction of Reform*, Kanishk Publishers and Distributor (2004).
8. *S.P Gupta* vs. *Union of India*, AIR 1982 SC 149.
9. *S.C. Advocate on Record* vs. *Union of India*, (1993) 4 SCC 441.
10. *Subhash Sharma* vs. *Union of India*, AIR 1991 SC 631.
11. In Re Presidential Reference, AIR 1999 SC 1.
12. K. Mahesh and Bishwajit Bhattacharya, *Judging the Judges*, Gyan Publication House (1999).
13. Nagender Sharma, "Probe against any judge should be confidential", *Hindustan Times*, 20/9/2012.
14 H.T. Correspondent, "Judges rush for post-retirement jobs not favourable", *Hindustan Times*, 1/10/2012.
15. Prashant Bhushan, "Judicial Accountability or Illusion", *Economic and Political Weekly*, November 2006.

16. S.P. Verma (ed.) "Indian Judicial System: Need and Direction of Reforms", Kanishka Publisher and Distributor (2004).
17. *Hussainara Khatoon* vs. *Home Secretary, State of Bihar* (1980) 1 SCC 8118.
18. S.M.N. Raina, *Law, Judges and Justice*, Vedpal Law House (1984).
19. Justice Shelat, 'Law, lawyers and judiciary', R. N. Shelat; distributors: New Gujarat Law House, 1972
20. T.P. Kelu, "For whom the judge is born", 2009(1) Kerela Law Times 50.
21. *Hussainara Khatoon* vs. *State of Bihar*, AIR 1979 SC 1360.
22. HT correspondent, "Pranab sounds warning on judicial activism", *Hindustan Times*, 9/9/2012.
23. S.P. Verma, "*Indian Judicial System*", Kanishka Publisher and Distributor (2004).
24. Shanti Bhusan, "Judicial Accountability Asset Disclosure", *Economic and Political Weekly*, September 12, 2009.
25. Arti Puri, " the Judges(Inquiry) Bill 2006 vis-à-vis accountability of higher judiciary in India", *M.D.U. Law Journal* 12(2) 2007, Vol. XII, part-II.
26. Rajeev Thukral, *Hindustan Times*, 20/03/2006.
27. T. Devida and Hem Lal Bhandari, "Judicial Accountability", *Journal of Indian Law Institute*, Vol. 88.1 2006.
28. Report of the All India Committee on Jail Reforms, 1980-83, Vol.1, para 12.2, p.170.
29. Hindu Correspondent, "Action of Judges under scanner", *The Hindu*, March 11, 2007.

□□□